This Journal Belongs to

_____

_____

(Date)

"Jen Norton's mastery of the symbolic power of color compels us to ponder anew the events leading to our redemption. Her art causes the scriptures to resonate prayerfully, leading us from simple meditation to mystical contemplation."

Elizabeth Lev
Vatican art historian and author of
How Catholic Art Saved the Faith

"In this unique artistic and contemplative journey through the Stations of the Cross you will see the passion of Christ in a whole new light. Norton's powerful writing will help you prayerfully unite yourself with Jesus on his journey to Calvary. A treasure for Lenten meditation or anytime."

Michele Faehnle
Coauthor of *Divine Mercy for Moms* and *Pray Fully*

"Every Lent, I attempt to follow the Stations of the Cross every week, and I have usually fallen away midway through the season! Jen Norton's journal has changed that for me. It offers so many avenues of prayer, contemplation, and discussion, I find myself fired up by this devotion in a whole new way. I know you will be, too!"

Allison Gingras
Catholic author and founder and host of *Reconciled to You*

Surrender All

An Illuminated Journal Retreat through the
STATIONS OF THE CROSS

Jen Norton

AVE MARIA PRESS AVE Notre Dame, Indiana

Founded in 1865, Ave Maria Press is a ministry of the United States Province of Holy Cross.

www.avemariapress.com

Paperback: ISBN-13 978-1-64680-007-0

Cover and interior artwork © Jen Norton.

Cover and text design by Katherine Robinson.

Printed and bound in Canada.

Contents

Preface vii

How to Use This Book xiii

Enter the Gate: Hosanna! 1

Station 1: Jesus Is Condemned to Death 9

Station 2: Jesus Takes Up His Cross 17

Station 3: Jesus Falls the First Time 25

Station 4: Jesus Meets His Mother 33

Station 5: Jesus Meets Simon of Cyrene 41

Station 6: Veronica Wipes the Face of Jesus 49

Station 7: Jesus Falls the Second Time 57

Station 8: Jesus Meets the Women of Jerusalem 65

Station 9: Jesus Falls the Third Time 75

Station 10: Jesus Is Stripped of His Garments 83

Station 11: Jesus Is Nailed to the Cross 91

Station 12: Jesus Dies 99

Station 13: Jesus Is Taken Down from the Cross 107

Station 14: Jesus Is Laid in the Tomb 115

In the Garden: Resurrection! 123

Acknowledgments 133

Appendix: Reflections for Walking the Stations 135

Preface

By the work, one knows the workman.

—*J. de La Fontaine*

Growing up in the 1970s, we always watched the *Jesus of Nazareth* TV miniseries during Lent. I would sit close to my mom on our goldenrod-yellow leather couch, riveted to the story. We watched as the narrative wound its way through the three years of his public ministry, when Jesus told us stories, demonstrated the Way of his kingdom, challenged authority and crowd mentality, and loved us unconditionally.

And then, as the timeline wound down to the final week and then to the last twenty-four hours of his earthly life, I stared at that thirteen-inch black-and-white television screen, both captivated and horrified. *How could someone betray Jesus? How could anyone hammer nails into another person? Why couldn't the Romans see how good Jesus was?* My young mind could not comprehend that kind of evil. But one thing I clearly understood: Jesus was willing to go all the way for me—and for each and every one of us.

When I decided to paint the Stations of the Cross, my objective was to prayerfully explore some of the emotions played out on that Good Friday. Using color and the placement of the Cross, I hoped to recapture some of that childhood awe. As I worked and each image took shape, I tried to enter more deeply into the scene, asking, *Where was the pain?*

Where was the grace? How does it all relate to modern life? To my life?

We all learn in different ways. I am a visual person. I miss a lot through sound. I am a horrible singer, have no talent for foreign language, and have to listen to sections of audiobooks over and over. But if I can see something, I get it. As one astute friend once revealed to me, visual language is my first language. English came second.

For me—and perhaps for you as well—making art is a form of prayer. Sitting with a story, using the colors, shapes, and textures of the visual language palette, we can experience the emotional story more clearly. And when that happens, we are better able to suspend judgment and think a bit more intuitively.

My hope with this series of work and this book is to give you another way to experience the story of the Via Dolorosa— one less about rational thought and more about feeling. If my artwork enables you to go deeper into your own reflection, you might find that God reveals something new in his invitation to you.

In Difficult Times

As this book was going into production, the COVID-19 pandemic hit, and our entire world changed overnight. Suddenly we found ourselves walking the Stations of the Cross together in a whole new way: stumbling, anxious, and suffering—but also helping, consoling, and showing mercy and compassion for one another.

When I originally painted these stations, I used neutral grays for the crowds along the Via Dolorosa. Perhaps if I were painting them again today, those grays would fracture into clearer darks and lights, reflecting the ways each of us figures out how to respond to the current crises. After the crisis began, I reread my words in this book, listening to whether or not they still rang true in such desperate times. In the face of real danger, did the ideas just feel like a made-up abstraction?

What I found was the stories and reflections are as relevant as ever. It is you, the reader, who will now take them in with a more immediate, concrete understanding. In a world hungering and thirsting for hope, it may be easier to recognize the suffering and risen Christ. He is right here . . . in the fear, the dying, the helping.

Do we recognize our oneness with him? Or do we stand aside, only preserving our own physical life? Probably a little of both, but it's something to ponder in prayer. It's a subject for reflection, repentance, and change.

Like the festival-goers at Passover, we didn't see this coming. For a time, our churches closed and the Body of Christ as we know it was hidden behind locked doors. Our hope faltered, and like Mary Magdalene, we may have asked, "Where have you taken my Lord?" (see Jn 20:13). We had to look elsewhere—to our neighbors, and within our own hearts—to find him. Some of us were called by name to participate in healing or consoling, such as the many health-care workers on the front line. Some of us may have sought his comfort as we walked our own road to Calvary. None of it has been easy, and we may not yet know where we fit in the scene.

Wherever our situation may be, we can be sure that Jesus is there with us. That is the promise he made by his sacrifice of body and blood: that he would always be with us, "until the end of the age" (Mt 28:20). May we never let our eyes deceive us. Hard times require seeing with the heart. Let us

move steadily forward through our deserts toward the life
he has promised us.

How to "Read" These Images

This series is intentionally more abstract and less illustrative
than most of my work. I've used specific colors to illustrate
some of the spiritual components.

- Red is used to indicate points of pain. Sometimes it is
  physical pain, like Jesus' hands and knees hitting stone as
  he falls. And sometimes it's emotional devastation, as in
  the sorrow shared with the women of Jerusalem.
- Blue represents the presence of God, Jesus' breath and
  life force.
- Neutral-toned areas represent the collective "us." For or
  against Jesus, we are somewhere in that crowd. It is up
  to each of us to decide how close we come or how far we
  stand back as he passes by.
- Black is the color of the cross, a deep black representing
  the weight of our sin. It changes position and direction
  depending on the narrative. As you go through the stations, notice when it separates Jesus from the crowd. Feel
  its overpowering reality when it is static and heavy and
  its violence when it is dynamically placed.
- White represents the Holy Spirit. It is worn by Jesus in his
  garments, until he is stripped of them in the tenth station.
  It is also present as tiny sprinkles throughout the series,
  showing up near the pain or in a connection with one of
  the secondary characters. It is only absent at his death.

As I worked on this series, I thought about what Jesus suffered just for me. I thought about the times I made his Cross heavier or the nails sharper with my sins. I thought about being part of the crowd and not speaking up to defend his innocence. I pondered what it must have been like for his mother, as only a mother could.

Making this series and then writing this book gave me a much deeper sense of gratitude for the graces I have received, especially in the mystery of the Eucharist—something that can get lost in a scientifically driven world. I hope that as you go through this book, you will also have occasion to pause and reflect on your own life and how Jesus has made himself present to you, especially in the Mass. He is the God who seeks us, comes to find us wherever we are, and invites us to his banquet table. Is something holding you back? Maybe pondering these pages of art and words will help you through your resistance to answer your call.

Making art is part inspiration, part divine intervention, plus a lot of discipline. Discipline is especially necessary when working on a series. It's easy to be excited about a new idea—and it can be tempting to lay it aside for something that brings back that high again. Don't give in to it! Take a deep breath, and keep going. Exploring every angle of an idea produces work of greater depth. Truth and beauty take time to fully manifest. As you persevere in the work, focusing on the task at hand rather than jumping from idea to idea, the extraneous falls away, revealing unexpected surprises.

What is true of the artist is also true for anyone who gazes upon the artwork. If you let yourself experience a work of art—both resting in the full image and spending time in particular details as they capture your imagination—you will receive the spirit of the artists' intent, and maybe even a further revelation in your heart.

Jesus' walk to Calvary and his death were necessary for us to fully understand God's work. We have to suffer death in order to partake in the resurrection. How far will we go to do the will of God? How much of our own selfish desire will we let die? How brave will we be in the face of evil? As you reflect on each station, ask yourself, *What will it take for me to surrender all?*

How to Use This Book

As the subtitle ("An Illuminated Journal Retreat through the Stations of the Cross") indicates, this book is designed to guide you through the classic Catholic devotion of the Stations of the Cross by engaging you in a creative journaling process. The word *illuminated* refers both to the use of light in each station image and to the spiritual light that you will receive as you ponder each image and reflection.

The "retreat" component of this book can be experienced in any number of ways: Individually, as part of your personal prayer during Lent or at any other time of personal struggle or sorrow. Use it as a guided family meditation during Holy Week, perhaps starting with the first chapter on Palm Sunday and reading two chapters each day until Easter Sunday (encouraging family members to use their artistic gifts to place themselves in the story). Parish groups can use the book as a Lenten offering by praying together the reflections in the Appendix. Additional resources including a Stations of the Cross poster for classroom use are available at JenNortonArtStudio.com.

Enter the Gate: Hosanna!

Exult Greatly
O daughter ZION!
Shout for JOY, O
Daughter Jerusalem!
Behold:
your King is Coming
to you
A just Savior is he
humble & riding on
a Donkey, on a colt
the foAL of a donkey.

ZECHARIAH 9:9

JN

A Scripture Reading

When they drew near Jerusalem and came to Bethpage on the Mount of Olives, Jesus sent two disciples, saying to them, "Go into the village opposite you, and immediately you will find an ass tethered, and a colt with her. Untie them and bring them here to me. And if anyone should say anything to you, reply, 'The master has need of them.' Then he will send them at once." . . . The disciples went and did as Jesus had ordered them. They brought the ass and the colt and laid their cloaks over them, and he sat upon them. The very large crowd spread their cloaks on the road, while others cut branches from the trees and strewed them on the road. The crowds preceding him and those following kept crying out and saying:

"Hosanna to the Son of David;
    blessed is he who comes in the name of the Lord;
hosanna in the highest."

—Matthew 21:1–3, 6–9

A Moment to Reflect

During the week of the Passover festival, the human story of Jesus would reach its climax and resolution, in fulfillment of the scriptures. Before leaving their safe encampment for Jerusalem, Jesus gathered his disciples and warned them of the dangers ahead: he was about to come face-to-face with evil in the heart of the Holy City, and it was God's will that—at least for a time—the powers of destruction would win.

At first Peter balked, wanting to protect his precious friend and teacher. But Jesus rebuked him: "Get behind me, Satan! . . . You are thinking not as God does, but as human beings do" (Mt 16:23).

One of Satan's best tricks is getting us to think that we are in control, that we can outthink God, that our own will should guide us. Jesus is directly confronting this lie as he lays forth the narrative of redemption. He is asking his closest disciples to walk *with* him, faithfully yoked to his Father's will.

Jerusalem would become the birthplace of a new kind of kingdom, not through might or political maneuvering, but through the shedding of innocent blood. And Jesus would enter this city of his new heritage in the same way his mother had carried him into Bethlehem, the place of his earthly father's origins: on a lowly beast of burden.

Upon Jesus' arrival, the crowds cheered and laid out a "red carpet" of cloaks and palm fronds. *What an exciting festival!* they must have thought. *Look! The powerful prophet Jesus is here to heal us!* And Jesus did come to heal—but not at all in the way they had imagined. By the end of the week, the people would see their acclaimed prophet crucified, dead, and buried. Faith would be shaken; allegiances would shift. Fear would take hold, and most would run away to escape this unexpected plan of healing and salvation they had celebrated such a short time before.

Jesus proceeds anyway, willingly offering himself as the ultimate sacrifice.

It's easy to see how the people didn't understand what was happening, and how they lost faith. They had no idea of how the story would end. We do, yet we can still find it hard to trust in God. We feel joyful and blessed when things go according to plan, but stumble and fall when they don't.

Like Peter, we must learn to walk with Christ, not ahead of him, as he lovingly forges our weaknesses into strengths, declaring us worthy despite ourselves. The depth of spirit we gain on our difficult roads assures us that the peace we attain in this life will not be taken from us in the next.

My Creative Illuminations

Before you proceed with this exercise, reread the gospel passage, taking note of the words and images that are particularly meaningful to you. You might choose to express these ideas creatively, using your favorite art supplies or a special notebook or journal. Once you have placed yourself in the story, take a few moments to reflect on the questions below.

"SURRENDER ALL" JOURNAL PROMPTS

Surrender to Jesus. Have I ever put my will before what I knew was right, as Peter did with Jesus? As I became self-aware of my behavior, what changes did I put in place so I wouldn't fall into the same trap again? What else did I learn from this experience?

Come to the silence. As I ponder the image of Jesus entering Jerusalem, what are my other senses telling me about what is going on in that moment? How does it sound, smell, and feel? In their jubilation, the crowd could not grasp what was truly happening. What can I do to shut out the noise and excitement of the secular world to be able to hear God clearly?

Make my faith real. What ways did my own family practice their faith, and what memories do I have from my own child-hood related to these practices that I would like to pass along to other members of my family and use to keep my own faith alive?

TURN UP THE LIGHT

Do you regularly welcome Jesus into your home, into your life? Begin a tradition of prayer and reflection with your family, or with a group of close friends. You might say the Rosary together, join or begin a prayer group, or even just examine your day together around the dinner table. Make a point to make this a regular part of your life.

Prayer for the Journey

Dear Jesus:

Help me trust you and walk in your understanding, not my own. When my head spins in worry over my hopes and fears, help me place my trust in you as loving Lord of my life. Let me walk with you, trusting you to set the pace as we take the steps together, one at a time. Help me not to rush ahead or insist on my own direction, but be open to your plan, which is far above my understanding. Protect my heart from questioning you as you lead me in your ways. *Amen*.

STATION 1

Jesus Is Condemned to Death

A Scripture Reading

As soon as morning came, the chief priests with the elders and the scribes, that is, the whole Sanhedrin, held a council. They bound Jesus, led him away, and handed him over to Pilate. Pilate questioned him, "Are you the king of the Jews?" He said to him in reply, "You say so." The chief priests accused him of many things. Again Pilate questioned him, "Have you no answer? See how many things they accuse you of." Jesus gave him no further answer, so that Pilate was amazed.

—Mark 15:1–5

A Moment to Reflect

Evil exists, and it is part of our human condition. Even with the best of intentions, our spines bend under the weight of fear, jealousy, shame, and pride. After the last Passover meal Jesus shares with his closest companions (see Lk 22:14–20), the story turns dark as the power of evil encroaches. Jesus is betrayed by a close friend, condemned by leaders of his own faith, and sentenced to death by a political opportunist. Giving in to mob mentality, the same crowd whose resounding Hosannas carried him into Jerusalem now publicly mock and condemn him. Jesus is utterly shunned and alone—heartbreakingly, soul-crushingly deserted.

Look back at the painting and see the splashes of red, which denote points of pain. In this station, Jesus is bound and powerless. The Lamb of God doesn't defend himself; he no longer heals, converts, or touches. The heavy, dark Cross walls off Jesus from the crowd, just as God's presence (in blue) seems to withdraw from him.

Note the flashes of red among the crowd as well. Some in that crowd knew he was innocent. Some were uncertain and didn't speak out. Many bystanders felt powerless against evil and condemned by their own fears. In condemning Jesus, in abandoning him to a cruel death, they also condemn themselves. And so do we.

It's so easy to believe that, in similar circumstances, we'd never condemn Jesus ourselves. But Jesus isn't just the compassionate teacher from the old TV miniseries. The real Jesus lives in us and among us. He's in the homeless, the immigrant, and the disabled. He is in the man who honors his wife, the woman who cares for her neighbor, the child who doesn't steal even when no one is looking. He is in the chaos of possibility and the order of discipline.

We all know the outcome of this story. It's so easy to want to jump ahead, to forget what this awful night was like. But to get to redemption, we must first confront and name the stone in our own hearts. We must take our place in this scene.

My Creative Illuminations

Before you proceed with this exercise, reread the gospel passage, taking note of the words and images that are particularly meaningful to you. Write or draw your impressions as you put yourself in the place of each character in the narrative. You might choose to express these ideas creatively, using your favorite art supplies or a special notebook or journal. Once you have placed yourself in the story, take a few moments to reflect on the questions below.

"SURRENDER ALL" JOURNAL PROMPTS

Can I surrender to injustice? Have I ever been unjustly condemned, like Jesus? Lied about, judged, shamed, or wrongly accused? How did I respond in those situations? Did I react or keep silent? If I had it to do over again, would I respond differently today?

Are my own hands clean? Have I ever "washed my hands" of responsibility, like Pilate, when I should have acted? Have I ever turned a deaf ear to the promptings of the Spirit, as Pilate turned from his wife's urgent messages?

Does my silence condemn me? Have I been a nameless face in the crowd, perpetrating an injury or simply going along with the crowd even though I have my doubts about the justice of the situation?

TURN UP THE LIGHT

When we are passionate about our beliefs, it is sometimes difficult to hear other points of view. Think of a particular issue that you feel strongly about, and write it down (in just a few words) on a clean sheet of paper. Next, write down all the reasons (whether or not you agree with them) someone might take the opposite view. Consider how our judgments are influenced by our beliefs, family, geography, or social status.

Prayer for the Journey

Dear Jesus:

You willingly faced pain, rejection, and hell itself to show me that there is more to your kingdom than what I can see or fully understand. Your love for me is personal. Help me clearly see my own faults, so I may reconsider my thoughts and actions. Let me see others as you see them, not through the lens of my judgments. Let your Spirit flow through me so I may find courage to stand, speak, think, and act in order to bring your kingdom of love to fruition. Protect me from my fears so that I may be delivered from doing evil. *Amen.*

STATION 2

Jesus Takes Up His Cross

A Scripture Reading

Who, though he was in the form of God,
    did not regard equality with God something
        to be grasped.
Rather, he emptied himself,
taking the form of a slave,
coming in human likeness;
and found human in appearance,
he humbled himself,
    becoming obedient to death,
    even death on a cross.

—Philippians 2:6–8

A Moment to Reflect

A cross is not an easy thing to carry. It's easy to forget in modern life, where we wear crosses as jewelry and hang them on our walls for decoration. But look at the altar in any Catholic church in the world, and you will be reminded of the rugged horror it presented in its heyday as a Roman torture device. It had to hold the weight of a man, so it must have been thick and heavy. You can bet nobody sanded it down, so it must have dug splinters into the victim's shoulders and hands. And it most certainly didn't have handles or wheels for easier transport.

A person sentenced to crucifixion had to carry the ultimate weapon of his demise uphill for about half a mile, in full view of a mob of town voyeurs. There was no relief—only shame, exhaustion, and ultimate death. The obvious pain and suffering were meant to deter anyone else from going against the rule of law. One would have to be crazy to risk the same.

But Jesus wasn't just anyone. He was the Son of God, and he had a mission to shoulder the weight of the world. He was, and is, a true King. Unlike most political rulers throughout history, he didn't demand that his subjects bow to his will. Rather, he bowed to God's will, surrendering everything for the sake of his subjects. He was revolutionary, countercultural. He was zealous, confrontational. And he was willing to accept the consequence of the Cross to show us he was also compassionate and obedient.

As he picks up his Cross, his shoulders ache and his hands sting. God's divine love, shown again in the blue of the halo, encircles him and grows radiant as he takes hold.

Sometimes a cross is thrust on us unjustly, such as a terminal illness or an undeserved sentence. Sometimes it comes with the choices we make in our work or personal lives. Our challenge in life is to work with what we are given, carry our cross faithfully, and allow the proverbial "fire" to forge us into something even more beautiful. Jesus knows how heavy a cross can be, and he will help us carry it.

My Creative Illuminations

Before you proceed with this exercise, reread the scripture passage, taking note of the words and images that are particularly meaning-ful to you. If you choose, make a collage of tangible images created or repurposed from magazines or other resources to display the feelings the passage from Philippians evokes in you. (You may find, as I do, that the physical touching and manual manipulation of the images—as opposed to the digital manipulation through an app such as Pinterest or Canva—is an important part of the editing process.) Once you have placed yourself in the story, take a few moments to reflect on the questions below.

"SURRENDER ALL" JOURNAL PROMPTS

Can I surrender myself to be emptied? God has created each of us for holiness. He often uses suffering as a way to empty us of pride or self-will and to turn our minds and hearts back to him. Can I think of a recent time of suffering, when I had no choice but to trust in God and stay close to him in prayer?

Does my love have limits? How far would I be willing to go for the good of someone I love? Is there a line I won't cross? Why or why not?

Reflect on the story of Maximillian Kolbe. The Franciscan friar is an iconic figure, best known for willingly exchanging his own life for that of a fellow prisoner in Auschwitz. (More of his story can be found at KolbeShrine.org). He wrote, "A single act of love makes the soul return to life." What do I think he meant?

TURN UP THE LIGHT

Make a "first response" jar. Fill an empty glass jar with slips of paper that contain the beginnings of prayers or quotes that prompt you to trust God when you are in doubt. The quotes may be from the Bible—a phrase from the Psalms or Proverbs—or from a Christian writer or speaker you admire. Pull one out whenever you are pondering something difficult, and see if it can lead you to consider first what God wants of you.

Prayer for the Journey

Dear Jesus:

You have created me in your image so that I may grow in holiness. I am also created of flesh, and physicality brings with it unavoidable weakness. There are crosses I don't want, crosses I trip over repeatedly, and burdens I blame wholly on others. Teach me to be obedient to your will. Help me to see the times when I must pick up the cross before me and bear the weight myself. Remind me that you are there to help me with the heavy lifting. *Amen*.

STATION 3

Jesus
Falls
the
First
Time

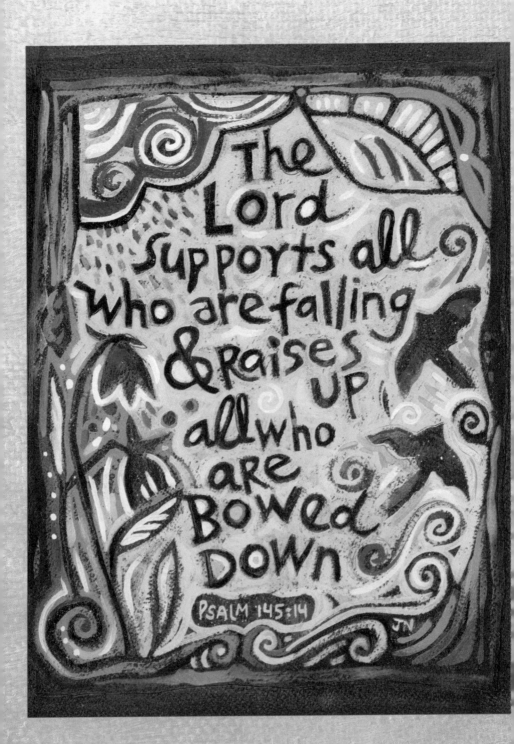

A Scripture Reading

Yet it was our pain that he bore,
    our sufferings he endured.
We thought of him as stricken,
    struck down by God and afflicted.
But he was pierced for our sins,
    crushed for our iniquity.
He bore the punishment that makes us whole,
    by his wounds we were healed.
We had all gone astray like sheep,
    all following our own way;
But the LORD laid upon him
    the guilt of us all.

—Isaiah 53:4–6

A Moment to Reflect

It's no accident that Jesus falls early in the stations. He had been up all night praying before being interrogated by the Sanhedrin and Pilate. After his conviction, he was beaten, mocked with a crown of thorns, and then forced forward bearing the heavy burden of the rugged Cross. His will, the will of his Father, was strong. But his flesh was weakening. He was tired. The forces of evil and gravity were pulling him down. If Jesus had been relying solely on human strength, that stumble and fall might have been the end. But his will was always aligned with the Father's, and the Spirit gave him strength to hold fast to his Father's redemptive plan.

Not so with us. Our will is so easily enticed along the wrong path, even with the best of intentions. Like children clamoring for the largest slice of cake at a birthday party, we can commit a thousand selfish acts every day without even realizing it. We love to pass the buck and simultaneously justify our actions, especially if no one else is looking. Time after time, we put our own desires above what is good for others, all the while acting "holier than thou."

Satan loves this, of course. We make it so easy on him. But we should be on watch for those small missteps. Each one moves us slightly out of line with our destination of holiness. Over time, they add up. Eventually we find ourselves on a path of "relativism," deaf to that still, small voice of the Spirit. This makes it much easier for the devil to lead some of us blindly into pits of self-pity, despair, and self-righteous pride, and to tempt others with bigger sins, causing injuries to the soul that are far more serious than knee scrapes. No, we must stay aware and disciplined in our ordinary steps if we are to continue to walk with Jesus.

My Creative Illuminations

Today's scripture reading evokes the familiar strains of George Frideric Handel's Messiah: *"Surely He Hath Borne Our Griefs" (no. 24). Before you proceed with this exercise, reread the passage. (You might also benefit from listening to a recording of Handel's rendition, available on YouTube). Take note of the words and images that are particularly meaningful to you. You might choose to express these ideas creatively, using your favorite art supplies or a special notebook or journal. Once you have placed yourself in the story, take a few moments to reflect on the questions below.*

"SURRENDER ALL" JOURNAL PROMPTS

Surrender the pain of the next step. Is there something I need to get done that I've been avoiding? What has been holding me back? How can I take the first step toward this goal today?

Take a small step toward holiness. What are some of the "small sins" I commit that inconvenience others or show disrespect to God? What is one way I can grow in spiritual discipline and self-awareness?

Don't let pride trip me up. Can I think of any good habits that have become a source of pride or that cause me to look down on others for not living up to my standards? How can I model a more holy lifestyle that keeps me close to Jesus, aware of my own weaknesses?

TURN UP THE LIGHT

When you catch yourself stumbling in some small way, doing or thinking something that is selfish or not of the character you wish to be, stop and say a prayer of gratitude for the awareness of this small sin. Consider sketching the knees of Jesus, bleeding from his journey toward the Cross. Create a border of black (representing our sins) and blue (the healing presence of the Spirit). Which is predominant in your picture? In your life?

Prayer for the Journey

Dear Jesus:

Keep me on the path you have set before me to do your will. I try to walk the way of holiness, but some days I am weak or tired, or just plain distracted by life. At those times, gently guide me back to behold your loving face, and remind me that my inheritance in your kingdom is far more important than my immediate happiness or physical convenience. Keep me ever aware that I must take your hand whenever I begin to stumble to avoid an even greater fall. *Amen.*

STATION 4

Jesus Meets His Mother

A Scripture Reading

And Mary said:
> "My soul proclaims the greatness of the Lord;
>> my spirit rejoices in God my savior.
>
> For he has looked upon his handmaid's lowliness;
>> behold, from now on will all ages call me blessed.
>
> The Mighty One has done great things for me,
>> and holy is his name.
>
> His mercy is from age to age
>> to those who fear him.
>
> He has shown might with his arm,
>> dispersed the arrogant of mind and heart.
>
> He has thrown down the rulers from their thrones
>> but lifted up the lowly.
>
> The hungry he has filled with good things;
>> the rich he has sent away empty.
>
> He has helped Israel his servant,
>> remembering his mercy,
>
> according to his promise to our fathers,
>> to Abraham and to his descendants forever."

—Luke 1:46–55

A Moment to Reflect

From the day her child is born, a mother begins to let go. First steps, first day at school, first heartache, first child of their own—a mother's selfless love lays the foundation for the life her child will lead. And, like Mary, mothers ponder. They see the connections between actions and emotions; they recognize the purpose of their children's lives drawn out over time. Attentive mothers will teach their children how to have compassion for themselves and others.

Yes, Jesus was God. But he was also fully human. Like every child, he was born innocent and helpless. As he grew, he needed proper direction from his parents in order to become all that he was meant to be. And now, on the road to Calvary, Mary experienced every mother's worst nightmare: her precious child at the mercy of destructive forces, in terrible pain, and dying a slow and shameful death. No amount of pondering could have prepared a mother for that heart-piercing experience.

Jesus sees his mother in the crowd and pauses. As their eyes meet, does he attempt to comfort her? Or does he crumble into her arms in tears? Is she strong, encouraging him with her presence and love? Or is she beside herself with heart-wrenching grief? Do each of them move on, step by painful step, reminding themselves that somehow all will be well, that God has not forsaken them? Each of these responses is possible.

Here, we see the Cross closing in on them, its oppressive heaviness suffocating them both. For the last moments of their fully human lives, mother and son are connected in a holy and momentary embrace. No words are recorded. Perhaps no words were necessary.

My Creative Illuminations

Before you proceed with this exercise, reread today's scripture reading, in which Mary proclaims an ancient Hebrew canticle you probably recognize as the Magnificat. Then look once more at the image of Jesus and Mary meeting. These two moments in the life of Mary—her joyous response to Elizabeth's affirmation of Mary's vocation, and her horror at the fulfillment of Simeon's prophecy (see Lk 2:34–35)—each required a mother's total surrender. Try to place yourself in the scene, and sketch or write about what you see. Once you have placed yourself in the story, take a few moments to reflect on the questions below.

"SURRENDER ALL" JOURNAL PROMPTS

Surrender the vision of motherhood. The word "mother" is not only a noun, but a verb. All women are called to mother in some way. Whom, and how, have I been called (or have I witnessed the call) to "mother"?

Consider Mary. What can I learn from Mary in how she mothered and loved Jesus? As I think of the women who have guided me into and through adulthood, those who have influenced the way I experience motherhood, do I see something of Mary in them too?

Encourage courageous motherhood. How do I "mother" others in my life and community? In a world geared toward undermining the value and desire of mothering, how do I encourage respect for that vocation in my family and my community? Am I willing to stand and face another's pain in order to ease their suffering? How is God calling me to do this?

TURN UP THE LIGHT

The pathway of suffering that took Jesus from Jerusalem to Golgotha covered just a few miles; the suffering of his body extends all the way around the world. Take an opportunity today to suffer as a mother does, standing courageously to ease the sufferings of others.

As you read the paper or watch the news on television, offer a Rosary for those—particularly children—subject to the world's temptations, dangers, and depravities. Pray especially for those who are separated from their mothers by violence or politics.

Prayer for the Journey

(FOR WOMEN)

Dear Jesus:

May I always value the essential role of mothers. As I spend time with you each day, keep me attentive to the needs of my children or others in my care—not only their physical needs, but their spiritual and emotional needs as well. Help me guide them in good times and in bad so that they see that all things work for the good and that no experience is wasted. Help me trust you with their care in all circumstances. As I love them, I know you love them even more. *Amen*.

(FOR MEN)

Dear Jesus:

As I spend time with you each day, keep me attentive to the needs of mothers and of all women. Let me live my days honoring the sacred role that women play in the shaping of each successive generation. Help me model what it means to encourage, affirm, and support them in that vital role. Thank you especially for my own mother, who helped me to become the man I am today, and for *your* mother, whose prayers for me keep me close to you as I make my way through this world. *Amen*.

Jesus Meets Simon of Cyrene

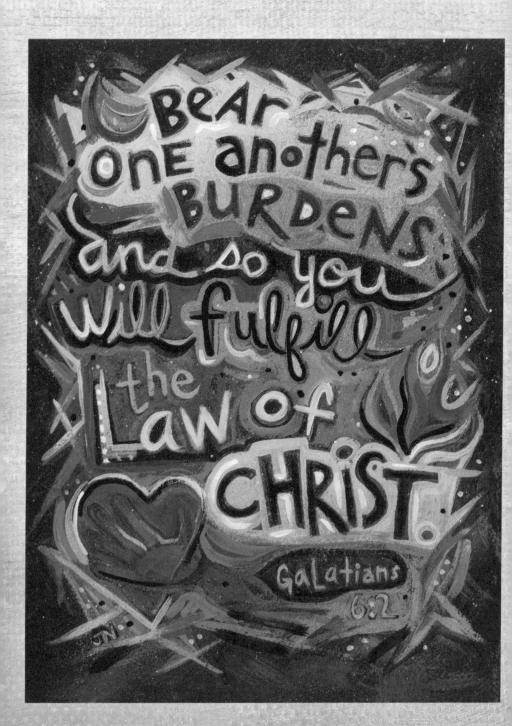

A Scripture Reading

They pressed into service a passer-by, Simon, a Cyrenian, who was coming in from the country, the father of Alexander and Rufus, to carry his cross.

—Mark 15:21

A Moment to Reflect

Jesus was physically broken. He was unable to carry his Cross any further, so the Roman guards looked around and grabbed the first strong guy they found to help: Simon of Cyrene.

Simon was a long way from home. Cyrene, Libya, is more than a thousand miles from Jerusalem. Perhaps he was there for work. Or maybe he was part of the Jewish population from Libya that came up for the Passover festival. Either way, he couldn't have known when he woke up that morning that he'd end up as a significant player in the spectacle of an execution—or that, two thousand years later, people around the globe would remember his name.

What was he thinking as the Roman soldiers approached? Did he look around at all the people swarming past him and wonder, *Why me?* Or did he recognize God's voice in the call of those soldiers and step forward willingly to do the work? True, he probably didn't feel like it, but on this day, love was shown through action.

Turn back to the image at the start of the chapter, and look at the colors again. As Simon carries the Cross with Jesus, notice how the red of pain is transferred to his part of the Cross. It was a thankless task that put him at the mercy of the soldiers, along with Jesus. But also notice how the negative space between their bodies becomes the shape of a heart, and the line of the Cross is much thinner and lighter within that act of love. Simon now bears the divine blue halo for his willingness to bear Jesus' burden. Simon probably did not feel the enormity of the Passion story he was entering. He may not have been fully aware of who Jesus was in this encounter. But on this day, Jesus was "the least of these" (see Mt 25:40), and Simon didn't turn away.

Simon's simple yes brought him close to Jesus and subsequently influenced his sons Alexander and Rufus, who were later known to the Christian communities. Thus, his work of mercy rippled out across time and space, reaching us even today.

God is big enough to find each of us right where we are. We cannot hide from his love. Yet he is also the gentle Father who calls to us through the longing of our hearts. We always have the choice to listen and follow, or to turn and run elsewhere. At times we are called to help; at other times, we are called to accept help gratefully. Either way, when we put aside our fears and hesitations, we are given the chance to understand the deep love of Jesus.

My Creative Illuminations

Before you proceed with this exercise, reread the gospel passage, taking note of the words and images that are particularly meaningful to you. You might choose to express these ideas creatively, using your favorite art supplies or a special notebook or journal. Once you have placed yourself in the story, take a few moments to reflect on the questions below.

"SURRENDER ALL" JOURNAL PROMPTS

Surrender to the call to receive. Have I ever experienced a time when, for whatever reason, I was unable to receive Communion, perhaps because the churches were closed? How did it affect the way I perceive the Real Presence of Christ in the Eucharist?

When I attend Mass now, do I feel like an outsider, or a full participant in the celebration? Do I understand that the Eucharist is the Real Presence of Jesus? If not, can I commit to learning more about this teaching?

Surrender to the call to serve. Simon the Cyrene stepped into his ministry when Jesus' body was broken. His actions may have been part of a deeper call to spread the faith to "the ends of the earth" (Ps 98:3). When I feel called by God to act, do I face reluctance? Why or why not? What change can I make in my heart so responding to that call would be easier next time?

Surrender to the call to love. How can I help carry a burden, or cross, for someone I know? Do I include the foreigner in this "call to love" the body of Christ?

TURN UP THE LIGHT

Think of a person who has help you in your life—a parent, a teacher, a friend. Write their name decoratively on a piece of art paper or canvas with a border around it. Make sure all shapes created by letters and negative shapes (spaces between letters) are fully enclosed so you can color them in. It's OK to trace computer-generated type if you don't want to draw freehand. Paint or color in the shapes of the name in a decorative way, sending that person gratitude, love, and light with each stroke.

Prayer for the Journey

Dear Jesus:

Help me hear and act on your invitation to bear witness to your presence to the world. Let me not take for granted your Real Presence in the Eucharist. You enter my very body, nourishing it with your love and demanding nothing of me. Help me understand the mystery of your Real Presence, and give me strength to answer your call to love you with my time, my talents, my treasures. *Amen.*

STATION 6

Veronica Wipes
the Face of Jesus

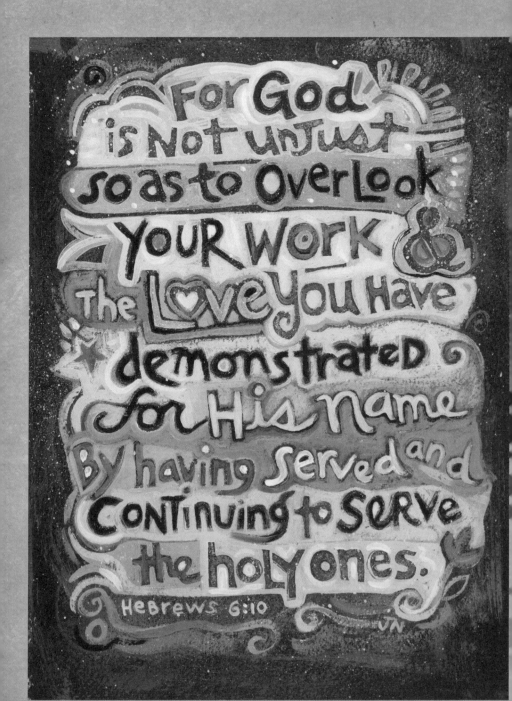

For God is Not unjust so as to overLook Your work & The Love You Have demonstrated for His name By having Served and Continuing to Serve the holy ones.

Hebrews 6:10

A Scripture Reading

They sent their disciples to him, with the Herodians, saying, "Teacher, we know that you are a truthful man and
that you teach the way of God in accordance with the
truth. And you are not concerned with anyone's opinion,
for you do not regard a person's status. Tell us, then, what
is your opinion: Is it lawful to pay the census tax to Caesar or not?" Knowing their malice, Jesus said, "Why are
you testing me, you hypocrites? Show me the coin that
pays the census tax." Then they handed him the Roman
coin. He said to them, "Whose image is this and whose
inscription?" They replied, "Caesar's." At that he said to
them, "Then repay to Caesar what belongs to Caesar and
to God what belongs to God." When they heard this they
were amazed, and leaving him they went away.

—Matthew 22:16–22

A Moment to Reflect

In the last station, we saw Simon pressed into service. He is probably like many of us: We are capable but, out of fear or a reluctance to be inconvenienced, we hold back from tending to the needs of the "least of these" until we are summoned to help.

In this station, we see a different response. Veronica willingly steps forward of her own accord. In a noisy, pressing crowd, it might have been hard for a woman to get near the center of the action—so easy it would have been to let the need pass by. In order to push through the crowd to reach Jesus, she would have had to summon both confidence and conviction. And yet, setting aside her own fears and excuses, she made her way up to his bloody, sweaty face to offer mercy and compassion using what was a significant part of her identity as a Middle Eastern woman: her veil. A veil was a powerful symbol, declaring to the world her marital and social status. Hers was an intimate act of care and concern.

Here we are reminded of all the women who played a strong supporting role in the Passion, beginning with Pilot's unnamed wife, who warned her husband not to involve himself in this drama over Jesus of Nazareth. Women's work often takes place behind the scenes but does not go unseen by

God. What society may overlook; God often rewards within the confines of our hearts.

According to tradition, when Veronica's veil was pulled away, a positive impression of Jesus' face was left on the fabric. Veronica's gift of love freely given is reciprocated with a tangible gift of grace. (Veronica's name is constructed of the Latin *veritas* and the Greek *icon*, literally meaning "true image.") Under Roman rule, all were obligated to pay their taxes using coins with Caesar's image imprinted on them. In this interaction with Veronica, Jesus offers us a new image for a new kingdom. Under the divine order of the Word of God, the face of Jesus, disfigured by our sin and imprinted on a garment of modest covering, strikes a new kind currency through an offering of selfless love.

My Creative Illuminations

Before you proceed with this exercise, reread both the gospel passage and the description of Veronica's act of love, taking note of the contrast between the two encounters: one of conflict and confrontation, the other of compassion and accompaniment. What do these two scenarios say to you about value and power? (If you have time, you might want to see the YouTube video from Catholic News Service of the exposition of St. Veronica's veil at St. Peter's Basilica.) Once you have placed yourself in the story, take a few moments to reflect on the questions below.

"SURRENDER ALL" JOURNAL PROMPTS

How do I relate to the story? Am I more like Simon or Veronica? Do I need to be asked, or do I step forward willingly? If the former, what is it that causes me to hold back?

What do I most value—and what am I reluctant to give? Jesus said, "For where your treasure is, there also will your heart be" (Mt 6:21). What do I worship? What is my highest priority in my decision-making? Are my decisions driven primarily by money or timetables or by human need?

How does what I believe line up with what I see and hear around me? Thinking of all the ads and slogans I've heard on the radio or television today, what is the predominant emotion they evoke? Fear? Pride? Greed? Anger? Hope? How can I begin to increase the good influences in my life and minimize the worldly and negative influences?

TURN UP THE LIGHT

Go online and look at various kinds of currency from around the world. What does it say to you about what is valued by that culture? If you were going to design the currency of the kingdom of God, what would it look like? If Jesus were to imprint his face on it, what would be the motto or slogan beneath his image?

Prayer for the Journey

Dear Jesus:

I owe you everything. You are the Word made flesh and the divine order to which I submit my entire being. I owe you a debt of love I can never repay. Let me never forget that I live, move, and have my being in you. Jesus, let me seek your face in everyone I encounter. Help me to freely offer my love and care to the least of your creation at all times. Deliver me from the fear that I am not worthy. *Amen.*

STATION 7

Jesus Falls the Second Time

Be Strong & take heart all who HOPE in the LORD

Psalm 31:25

A Scripture Reading

Then the scribes and the Pharisees brought a woman who had been caught in adultery and made her stand in the middle. They said to him, "Teacher, this woman was caught in the very act of committing adultery. Now in the law, Moses commanded us to stone such women. So what do you say?" They said this to test him, so that they could have some charge to bring against him. Jesus bent down and began to write on the ground with his finger. But when they continued asking him, he straightened up and said to them, "Let the one among you who is without sin be the first to throw a stone at her." Again he bent down and wrote on the ground. And in response, they went away one by one, beginning with the elders. So he was left alone with the woman before him. Then Jesus straightened up and said to her, "Woman, where are they? Has no one condemned you?" She replied, "No one, sir." Then Jesus said, "Neither do I condemn you. Go, [and] from now on do not sin any more."

—John 8:3–11

A Moment to Reflect

One can imagine the scene: A half-naked woman, dragged from the very bed in which her affair had been discovered, is standing in the middle of a circle of angry men. And where is the one she was with? Did he run off? We don't know. This story centers around the most helpless person, the scapegoat with virtually no voice: the woman. And where is Jesus? He appears among the men and is handed the power to convict. The wolves have circled, hungry for blood and justification. They are ready to fall upon the prey.

Notice that Jesus doesn't say not to stone her, or even that stoning her is wrong or that their wrath is unjustified. He upholds the law. He merely specifies who should throw the first stone: the one without sin. As he silently writes in the sand, the passage says each man went away, one by one, beginning with the elders. They didn't leave in a group, or with a companion, but alone. Interesting.

We don't know exactly what Jesus was writing. It could have been the Mosaic Law—the scribes and Pharisees would have been well-versed in it and recognized their own sins as they saw them written down. Or maybe he was writing specific indiscretions. Perhaps as each one recognized his own fallen state, written by the only one with true authority to convict, they chose to leave silently, not wishing to discuss their faults with their peers. And why the elders first? They had the hindsight of age. It's easier to justify wrong when you haven't lived long enough to see the consequences of your actions. It's a much more brutal conviction when you've had years to reflect and realize you are much closer to your own day of atonement.

Now the woman faces only Jesus, the man without sin. She has broken the law and expects a consequence. He is within his right to throw a stone. However, he hasn't come here to convict, but to offer salvation. He knows we all fall, unable to stand against the power of our own human desires. Maybe we even need to fall in order to view life from a different vantage point. Jesus meets the woman in the middle of her mess and shame and offers her liberation. He sees her whole story, not just one fallen moment. He only asks that she use this gift wisely and not sin again. She doesn't know it, but he will take the fall for her against that angry circle of men. That's what true love does.

My Creative Illuminations

Today's scripture is a powerful one, giving each of us an opportunity to see ourselves—perhaps relating to the woman, facing the angry accusers, or maybe recognizing our own tendency to cast hasty judgment, as these men did. Before you proceed with this exercise, reread the gospel passage, taking note of the words and images that are particularly meaningful to you. You might choose to express these ideas creatively, using your favorite art supplies or a special notebook or journal. Once you have placed yourself in the story, take a few moments to reflect on the questions below.

"SURRENDER ALL" JOURNAL PROMPTS

Surrender to God's mercy. In the times I have fallen away from Jesus and sinned, do I feel I can be forgiven, or do I still carry the stone of conviction? What is my reaction to the exchange between Jesus and the woman caught in adultery? What do I think God is saying to me here?

Forgive as I have been forgiven. Am I quick to judge others? How does it make me feel afterward? Do I struggle with offering forgiveness in any of my relationships? Can I see a person's fault in the context of his or her whole life, and can I pray for their well-being even as I hold my feelings?

Consider the sacrament of Reconciliation. Why is it harder to vocalize my faults and failings to a listening priest rather than just apologize in my own head? When I receive the sacrament, how do I feel, and is there an experience of grace?

TURN UP THE LIGHT

Create or repurpose a symbol of forgiveness that you can wear, carry, or place somewhere to be reminded daily that you can be forgiven. This can be an elaborate and decorative piece (such as a beautiful bracelet adorned with a cross), a religious item (such as a scapular or rosary), or a handmade and simple token (such as a stone imprinted or carved with a cross, or even a sticky note on your bathroom mirror). Use it as a daily reminder to go and sin no more.

Receive the sacrament of Reconciliation if you have not done so recently.

Prayer for the Journey

Dear Jesus:

I am sorry for having offended you in my thoughts, words, and actions. I am sorry for judging others without first examining my own brokenness. I ask for your forgiveness and want to be reconciled to you. I kneel before you, my King, and thank you for having taken the fall for my evil deeds and loving me still. Help me trust that you love me and will not condemn or shame me when I ask for your forgiveness. Help me to avoid sin from this day on. *Amen.*

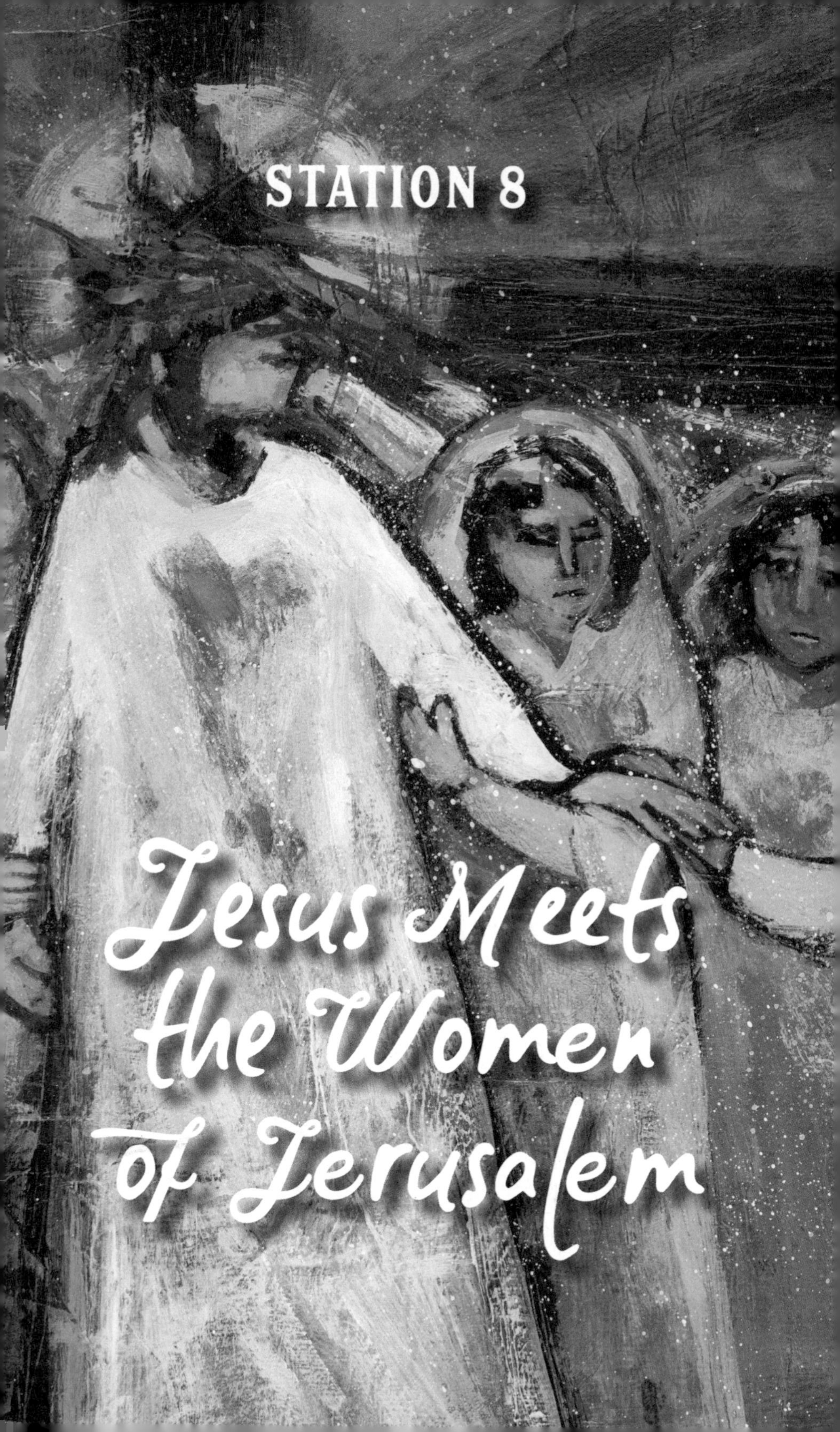

STATION 8

Jesus Meets
the Women
of Jerusalem

The Woman answered the Snake, "We may Eat of the fruit of the trees in the Garden; it is only about the fruit of the Tree in the middle of the garden that GOD Said 'You SHALL NOT eat it or even Touch it, or else you will DIE'"

GENESIS 3:2-3

JN

A Scripture Reading

Jesus turned to them and said, "Daughters of Jerusalem, do not weep for me; weep instead for yourselves and for your children, for indeed, the days are coming when people will say, 'Blessed are the barren, the wombs that never bore and the breasts that never nursed.' At that time people will say to the mountains, 'Fall upon us!' and to the hills, 'Cover us!' for if these things are done when the wood is green what will happen when it is dry?"

—*Luke 23:28–31*

A Moment to Reflect

Long ago, Satan calculated that if he could control the heart of a woman, he might command all of God's creation. That's how important women are to salvation. Women are the portal through which humans come into being. In the Garden of Eden, he sowed doubt into the woman's mind to erode her trust in God. She began to believe that the One who created her with a holy purpose was holding out on her.

The evil one twisted her innate desire to be loved and valued and planted seeds of doubt to make her question God's faithfulness. The mistrust that began between Eve and God spread to all her relationships. Adam followed her into doubt and joined her in sin. He should have reminded her that they already had all they needed in God. Instead, he became complicit in Satan's lies, ultimately blaming her for his own lack of prudence. With both partners hiding in shame from their Creator, an antagonistic seed was planted into the divine order. Broken trust: a simple but brilliant plan by the devil that has played out over and over again through time.

Women have the honor of carrying life within their very bodies. Yet Satan twists that into something shameful and inconvenient. Innocent love gets distorted to objectification. Personal interests, power, and profits are celebrated over life itself. Compassion and empathy, intrinsic to a woman's very nature, are redefined as weak and pitiable. As the woman's place of honor as a daughter and keeper of life has been devalued, children are viewed as liabilities and women are treated as second-class citizens. The consequence is that women and creation have been used, abused, and treated as lesser property, all in the name of other gods. And when women don't know their own worth, how can they possibly help men stay true to their own holy call to care for creation?

All this confusion, dehumanization, and environmental disorder springs from that same seedbed of lies planted by the evil one. And in this gospel passage, as Jesus sees the women of Jerusalem and validates their agony, Satan's falsehoods are exposed and the truth of God's love for the human race is unmistakably proclaimed.

In the artwork, Jesus' body is the center point of solidarity, creating the shape of a mountain or a buttressed cathedral as the women lean into him. The darkness of the Cross is weighing heavily behind them, but his halo rises before it like a divine sun. Red pain flows across the collective figures as his heart breaks for the choices and afflictions he knows they will face. The societal marginalization they endure under their feminine mantles is echoed in his bloody crown. As the world rejects him, so it also rejects the women.

All is not lost, for Jesus is relentless in his pursuit of our redemption. And as he looks upon our sisters, standing there along the Via Dolorosa, he sees us too. We can take heart that we are seen and uncompromisingly loved by our true King. He gave all on the Cross for us. We can trust him, even in the face of obstacles.

My Creative Illuminations

"If these things are done when the wood is green what will happen when it is dry?" This single line from today's scripture reading gives us ample food for thought. How would you describe your interior life right now—is it green and vibrant, or fading into dryness? The difference is the presence of water. How close are you staying to the Living Water? Before you proceed with this exercise, reread the gospel passage, taking note of other words and images that are particularly meaningful to you. You might choose to express these ideas creatively, using your favorite art supplies or a special notebook or journal. Once you have placed yourself in the story, take a few moments to reflect on the questions below.

"SURRENDER ALL" JOURNAL PROMPTS

Surrender my heart to God. A popular quote states: "A woman's heart should be so hidden in God that a man has to seek Him just to find her." What does this mean to me, personally? Are my desires oriented to God's will?

Consider the complementarity of men and women. Does my idea of "feminism" include the conviction that women are "just like men"? This is very common in contemporary society. The real question is: What did God intend when he created us "male and female" (Gn 5:1–2; Mk 10:6)? How do men and women complement each other by possessing different qualities, so they can be in accord, much like notes in a musical harmony?

Reflect on feminine beauty. How has the strength and power of women been diminished by objectification of their physical beauty? How might I creatively retell a traditional Bible story from the female perspective (for example, the story of Bathsheba from her point of view, not David's)? Reflecting on the experiences of the women in these stories, what do I think has changed or not changed for women through the ages?

TURN UP THE LIGHT

What can you do today—right now, even—to support a
pro-life organization that works to help women who face
unplanned pregnancies, who want to adopt, or who are stuck
in trafficking?

One of the most important ways—besides supporting
them financially—is to pray. So many women are suffering
in hidden places and feel forgotten and rejected by the whole
world. Some of them are pregnant and don't know what to
do. But just as Jesus saw the women in Jerusalem, he sees
you struggling with the challenges of your life, and he sees
those women, too. Your challenge today is to post this prayer
somewhere you will see it every day, and to offer it each day
for nine months on behalf of a woman you do not know, and
her child who needs you.

> Jesus, Mary and Joseph, I love you very much. I beg you to
> come to the assistance of the vulnerable pregnant woman
> who feels alone today. Help her and give her the hope she
> needs to spare the life of her child, the unborn baby who is
> in danger of abortion. By your Spirit, speak hope to their
> hearts today. *Amen*.

Prayer for the Journey

Dear Jesus:

You have crafted me with wonderful and fearful care. You have given me a role in bringing about your kingdom on earth. Inspire me with a spirit of stewardship, and remind me that I am good enough and strong enough for the purpose you have set forth for me. You have created every human life for a purpose, and you love each person as a unique and unrepeatable expression of his love in the world. Help me to be mindful that you are the author of all life, and give me eyes to see that all beings are part of your holy body and deserve care. Keep me from being derailed by the devil's lies: pride, greed, lust, envy, gluttony, wrath, and sloth. His reign will end; yours will not. Jesus, help me live in a way that reflects your incredible love for me. *Amen*.

STATION 9

Jesus Falls the Third Time

A Scripture Reading

Where do the wars and where do the conflicts among you come from? Is it not from your passions that make war within your members? You covet but do not possess. You kill and envy but you cannot obtain; you fight and wage war. You do not possess because you do not ask. You ask but do not receive, because you ask wrongly, to spend it on your passions. Adulterers! Do you not know that to be a lover of the world means enmity with God? Therefore, whoever wants to be a lover of the world makes himself an enemy of God. Or do you suppose that the scripture speaks without meaning when it says, "The spirit that he has made to dwell in us tends toward jealousy"? But he bestows a greater grace; therefore, it says:

> "God resists the proud,
>   but gives grace to the humble."

So submit yourself to God. Resist the devil, and he will flee from you. Draw near to God, and he will draw near to you. Cleanse your hands, you sinners, and purify your hearts, you of two minds. Begin to lament, to mourn, to weep. Let your laughter be turned into mourning and your joy into dejection. Humble yourselves before the Lord and he will exalt you.

— James 4:1–10

A Moment to Reflect

As we prayerfully follow Jesus' way to Calvary, we are given three chances to examine the nature of a fall.

The Way of the Cross is an unbearably difficult one for us humans. Our very essence embodies the disability of frailty. No matter how willing the spirit, our flesh can and will fail us. Perhaps we act out, mindlessly numbing pains and resentments, or we are compulsively drawn to a destructive activity in an attempt to fill an emptiness in our soul. We earthen vessels can get horribly cracked and broken.

If you have gone through something really big, really life-altering, you may have reached that point where there was nothing left but prayer. That's not a bad thing! Prayer is the resin that can fill those soul ruptures and make us whole again. When we fall to our knees, crushed by sin or depleted of strength, our only view is up. It is only after burning every bridge and exhausting every idea that we reach rock bottom and can gaze up at the Cross whole-heartedly, humbly and meekly crying, "Help me, Jesus."

Falling may be a necessary part of our life. When we become aware of our own shortcomings and finally submit to God's will, we are gifted with grace, the help we so desire. Not only are we forgiven, but we find God's grace to be sufficient for us to soldier on. Our fragile souls expand and are fortified as we see that Jesus has been there all along, waiting in the surrender. In that moment, the devil is defeated, and hope conquers despair.

My Creative Illuminations

Before you proceed with this exercise, reread the scripture passage from the Letter of James, taking note of the words and images that are particularly meaningful to you. You might choose to express these ideas creatively, using your favorite art supplies or a special notebook or journal. Once you have placed yourself in the story, take a few moments to reflect on the questions below.

"SURRENDER ALL" JOURNAL PROMPTS

Surrender to the Cross. In each of the art pieces for the three falls, the Cross has taken a more dynamic pose. In this third fall Jesus' figure is more visibly crushed, almost to the point of full surrender. Have I felt that devastated at times? Whom did I turn to for help? Were my prayers answered?

Look up in hope. Although we are all fallen, we all have hope in the Lord. What do I imagine it will be like to see Jesus face-to-face? Would I be ready if that day were today? Why or why not?

Jesus has often chosen the broken people of the world to evangelize his message, beginning with Peter. Do I consider this when I encounter someone who I know has done great wrongs?

TURN UP THE LIGHT

St. Teresa of Calcutta (Mother Teresa) sometimes said, "Peace begins with a smile." We can often sense when people around us are having a bad day—or a bad life—when they are rude or inconsiderate. Try offering a smile in line at the grocery store or letting someone pass in front of you on the road, and see if it changes the mood.

Prayer for the Journey

Dear Jesus:

My spirit is willing, but I am afraid. I do not feel suffi-ciently strong enough to walk with this pain. When I fall and when I am tempted to walk back down the rocky hill and away from you on the Cross, strengthen my resolve. Fortify me with hope in your promises. Fill my soul with your love and Divine Mercy. *Amen.*

STATION 10

Jesus Is Stripped of His Garments

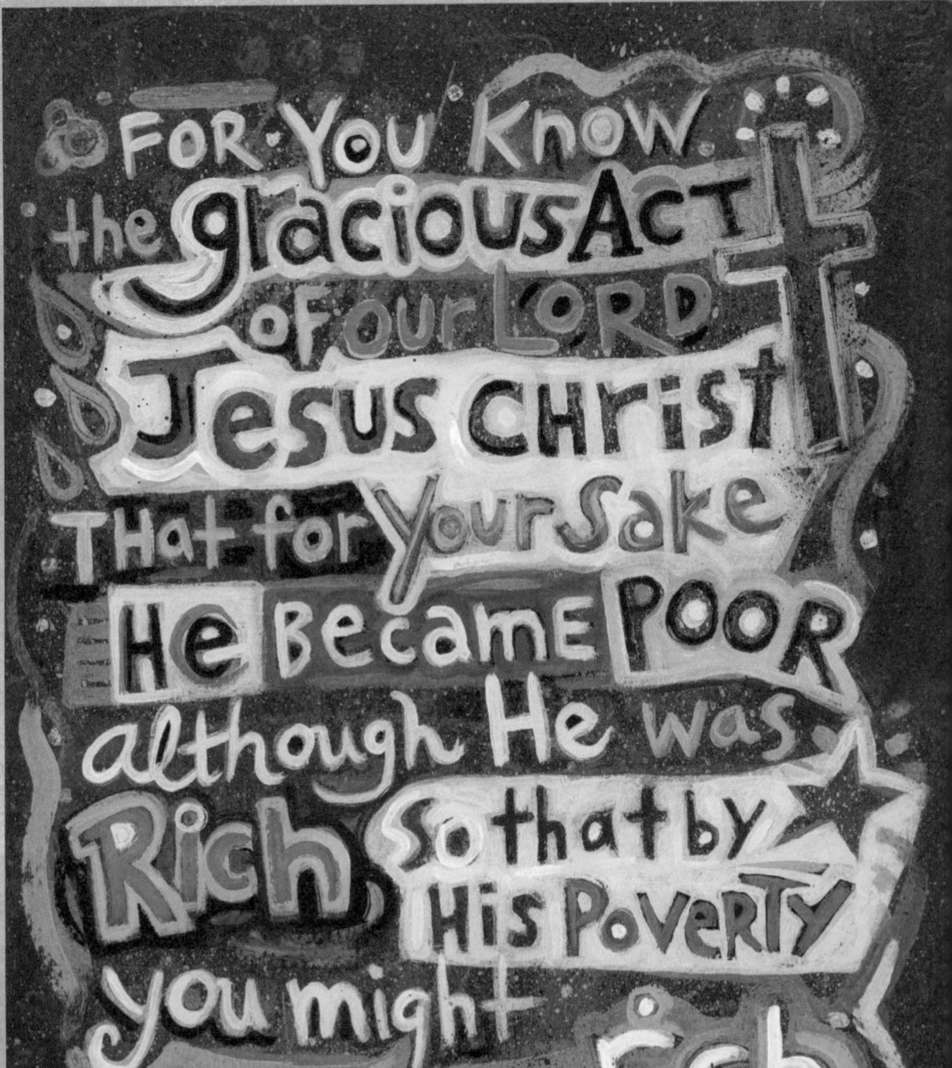
FOR YOU KNOW
the gracious ACT
of our LORD
JESUS CHRIST
THAT for your sake
HE BECAME POOR
although He was
Rich, so that by
His POVERTY
you might
become rich
JN
2 COR. 8:9

A Scripture Reading

When the soldiers had crucified Jesus, they took his clothes and divided them into four shares, a share for each soldier. They also took his tunic, but the tunic was seamless, woven in one piece from the top down. So they said to one another, "Let's not tear it, but cast lots for it to see whose it will be," in order that the passage of scripture might be fulfilled [that says]:

"They divided my garments among them,
    and for my vesture they cast lots."

This is what the soldiers did.

—*John 19:23–24*

A Moment to Reflect

In this final act of shaming, Jesus is stripped of his only earthly possessions and ceases to hold any social classification other than that of the cast-out scapegoat. He is mocked and exposed in the most demeaning way possible, robbed of any definition of self. To his persecutors, and to the mocking crowds that surround him, he is nothing.

But wait. Let's take a look at what they did with his stolen clothing. As they brutally tortured and murdered this man, the soldiers seemed to take great care with his belongings. The clothes must have been bloody and dirty from the arduous journey up the hill. Yet they don't discard them. Unknowingly fulfilling scripture (Ps 22:19), the soldiers carefully divide them among themselves and decide to keep one seamless undergarment intact.

Clothing, both then and now, determines a person's social status. Jesus' clothing conveys something of his nature to the world. Scripture says his tunic was "woven in one piece from the top down." This is significant because everyday Palestinian tunics most commonly would have been made of two pieces sewn together. The garment that Jesus wore would have required skill to make and was probably specially made for him.

Also significant is the seamless garment's connection with the priesthood of the old covenant. In John's Greek translation, his use of the word *hypodytes* for the seamless woven garment worn under Jesus' clothing correlates with the inner garment or tunic worn under a Levitical priest's *ephod*, or outer robe (see Ex 28:4), something Aaron was to wear as he entered the Holy of Holies on the Day of Atonement (Yom Kippur).

We see the significance of this after Jesus dies, when the "veil of the sanctuary was torn in two from top to bottom" (Mt 27:51). Like his tunic, the veil would have been seamless; its rending signifies a divine action from heaven to earth, God to man. The meticulous observations and sacrificial offerings of the ancient covenant are no longer needed. A new unbreakable covenant, signified by the untorn garment of Christ, is now established: Jesus, the true High Priest, has atoned for our sins once and for all. Now each one of us can partake of the sacrificial offering: his very Body and Blood, in the Eucharist.

My Creative Illuminations

Before you proceed with this exercise, reread the gospel passage, taking note of the words and images that are particularly meaningful to you. You might choose to express these ideas creatively, using your favorite art supplies or a special notebook or journal. Once you have placed yourself in the story, take a few moments to reflect on the questions below.

"SURRENDER ALL" JOURNAL PROMPTS

Surrender attachments. Am I defined by my money, clothing, or station in life? What would happen if these things went away?

Strip away assumptions. When I look at someone who has less than me, how do my words and actions reflect their dignity—or do I see them as less deserving of love or worth?

Embrace the sacramental life. The man who won the drawing for Christ's tunic likely did not realize the gift he had just received. We do not know who he was, or what became of the garment. What do I imagine happened to it? Do I cherish any blessed articles I have in my home and use them intentionally and meaningfully to stay connected to God and the Communion of Saints?

TURN UP THE LIGHT

Today we pray for priests, clergy, and world leaders. The next time you attend Mass, notice the altar decorations and colors. What do they say about the importance of what takes place there? Decorate your home with something that matches the colors of the liturgical season.

Prayer for the Journey

Dear Jesus:

Help me to let go of my attachment to things. When I lose the things that are dear to me, or that define who I am in the world, remind me that underneath it all I am still whole and enough. In you, I live and move and have my being. Nothing worldly can take your love from me, ever. Help me to use what I have to show others how much you love us all. *Amen*.

STATION 11

Jesus Is Nailed to the Cross

Take CARE BROTHERS, that none of You may have an evil & unfaithful heart so as to forsake the Living GOD

HEBREWS 3:12

A Scripture Reading

When the hour came, he took his place at the table with the apostles. He said to them, "I have eagerly desired to eat this Passover with you before I suffer, for, I tell you, I shall not eat it [again] until there is fulfillment in the kingdom of God." Then he took a cup, gave thanks, and said, "Take this and share it among yourselves; for I tell you [that] from this time on I shall not drink of the fruit of the vine until the kingdom of God comes." Then he took the bread, said the blessing, broke it, and gave it to them, saying, "This is my body, which will be given for you; do this in memory of me." And likewise the cup after they had eaten, saying, "This cup is the new covenant in my blood, which will be shed for you.

"And yet behold, the hand of the one who is to betray me is with me on the table; for the Son of Man indeed goes as it has been determined; but woe to that man by whom he is betrayed."

—Luke 22:14–22

A Moment to Reflect

Jesus was nailed to the Cross less than twenty-four hours after this scene transpired in the Upper Room. He had gathered with his closest friends, welcoming them and saying to them, "I have eagerly desired to eat this Passover with you before I suffer" (Lk 22:15). One can imagine him embracing each apostle with a heartfelt bear hug as he entered. It speaks to his great love that even in knowing he would soon be betrayed by a friend and be put to death by the leaders of his own faith, he is still able to focus on the celebration at hand. Later he will be praying in agony on the Mount of Olives, but for now he chooses to be fully present with his friends, sharing the traditional meal and confiding his final words of love and wisdom to them. Eleven of them listened intently, hearts full as their rabbi spoke. One person did not.

Judas had already conspired to hand Jesus over to the Jewish leaders and was preoccupied with his own task. Did he resent Jesus' popularity? Was he swayed by empty rationales or money? Did he want the approval of the Jewish elite? The stories vary, but what we do know is that, on this night, his heart was hardened toward the voice of his shepherd, and he chose the heresy of choosing his will over God's.

It is a gut-wrenching experience to be betrayed, especially by one you called "friend." That rejection and subsequent condemnation now plays out in physical, excruciating pain as Jesus is nailed to the Cross. Our delusions of self-righteousness and pride are pounded into his flesh. The hurt, betrayal, selfishness, and blasphemies of our guilt are as heavy as the lead nails. We can see clearly how our collective evil fixes him to the rugged Cross, how we have sealed his fate with our sinfulness. He reaches out, his eyes begging us to turn to him, but he cannot embrace us. We have averted our eyes and turned away. Our sin has him pinned down and keeps him at arm's length.

Later, when the nails are removed and lie rusting on the ground, the light of his Divine Mercy will shine through the holes in his hands. We can take solace that even with everything we have done and failed to do, in our thoughts and words, Jesus still chooses to remain in solidarity with us in his last moments, crying out, "Father forgive them, they know not what they do" (Lk 23:34). We killed the one who loved us most. We murdered the one who only wanted to call us to the banquet. And even so, Jesus has always been, is now, and forever will be on our side.

My Creative Illuminations

Before you proceed with this exercise, reread the gospel passage, taking note of the words and images that are particularly meaningful to you. You might choose to express these ideas creatively, using your favorite art supplies or a special notebook or journal. Once you have placed yourself in the story, take a few moments to reflect on the questions below.

"SURRENDER ALL" JOURNAL PROMPTS

Surrender to the eternal offering of love. Are there areas of my life where I am deliberately turning away from Jesus? What keeps me from reaching out to him?

Appreciate the Mass. When I attend Mass, am I fully there? Or am I mentally ruminating over my outside life? How can I better consider Mass as a "theater of heaven," a safe haven from the outside world?

Enter into the Divine Mercy. The Divine Mercy image portrays Jesus with rays of light emanating from his heart. In the famous diary of St. Faustina, she recounts her visions of Divine Mercy. Here is one passage: "I cannot punish even the greatest sinner if he makes an appeal to My compassion, but on the contrary, I justify him in My unfathomable and inscrutable mercy" (*Diary*, 1146). How does this description of Jesus' deep love and mercy for all sinners make me feel?

TURN UP THE LIGHT

This exercise is intended to help you reflect on the sins and thoughts that keep you at arm's length from your Savior. Paint a block of wood with a large, dark cross. Then paint streams of red and white (for blood and water) in a decorative way to represent the life of Jesus poured out for you. Pound a nail into the wood for each incident you think of, beginning at the four endpoints of the cross. This can be an ongoing project, done over months or years as you examine your life and heart. In the end, you will have an art piece and a reminder to "sin no more."

Prayer for the Journey

Dear Jesus:

Help me to dread the very thought of sin, or of doing anything that adds to your agony. When I am tempted to follow my own will instead of yours, help me remember that each indiscretion, big or small, takes me further from your embrace and causes you pain. My works do not go unseen by your eyes; the motivations of my heart will determine if I will live in your light in the next life, or if I have exhausted my happiness in this one. Keep me from believing any of Satan's empty promises and from giving in to temptations to despair. Remind me humbly to run to your open arms and ask for your Divine Mercy when I stumble. *Amen.*

STATION 12

Jesus Dies

Into your hands I commend my spirit; You will redeem Me Lord God of Truth

Psalm 31:6

A Scripture Reading

From noon onward, darkness came over the whole land until three in the afternoon. And about three o'clock Jesus cried out in a loud voice, *"Eli, Eli, lema sabachthani?"* which means, "My God, my God, why have you forsaken me?" Some of the bystanders who heard it said, "This one is calling for Elijah." Immediately one of them ran to get a sponge; he soaked it in wine, and putting it on a reed, gave it to him to drink. But the rest said, "Wait, let us see if Elijah comes to save him." But Jesus cried out again in a loud voice, and gave up his spirit.

—Matthew 27:45–50

A Moment to Reflect

In the Gospel of Luke we read: "Jesus cried out in a loud voice, 'Father, into your hands I commend my spirit'; and when he had said this he breathed his last" (23:46). Now Jesus, the most humble servant, is dead. Colors pale and the sky darkens as the last bit of life drips from this sacrificial lamb.

All Jesus has ever wanted is for us to accept his invitation to his kingdom—one ruled by unconditional, radical love. Behold the King who was even willing to die to save us. Other prophets and teachers may have shown us ways to worship or live peacefully, but Jesus, the true Messiah—with a capital *M*—is the only one who comes to find us in the deepest, darkest parts of ourselves. God from God, Light from Light, he is the begotten true God who calls us away from a life of deceit and heartache to one of compassion and joy. He is the link between heaven and earth, the "Way" now clearly hanging from a post like a directional sign.

Satan works to blind us from this truth. But he cannot create from nothing. He can only use our weaknesses and fragile egos to turn our view from Jesus to a lesser, unmarked path to nowhere. He says, "Look at that pitiable creature," never revealing that to give his very life for us was Jesus' plan all along. He is the horizontal beam, holding Jesus' hands to the wood, offering nothing. At the intersection of these two beams of opposing direction, we have the Cross.

It is finished. Scripture is fulfilled. The lamb is slain; the grain of wheat has fallen to the ground. Jesus' body and blood are offered for the life of the world.

My Creative Illuminations

Reread the gospel passage, taking note of the words and images that are particularly meaningful to you. You might choose to express these ideas creatively, using your favorite art supplies or a special notebook or journal. Once you have placed yourself in the story, take a few moments to reflect on the questions below.

"SURRENDER ALL" JOURNAL PROMPTS

Surrender to the Word of God. Even in his agony, Jesus' final lament to his Father echoed the scriptures he learned as a child, even as he gave up his last breath. His cry, "My God, my God, why have you forsaken me?" is from Psalm 22, which ends with notes of hope. How might have Mary responded to hearing this familiar psalm on the lips of her son?

Look at the art. Jesus' body hangs as gravity pulls him away from the wood and back down to earth. All of his physical existence is gone. Simultaneously, his body is in a form of a bird in flight. How would I describe the transition between life and death in light of Psalm 22?

TURN UP THE LIGHT

Pray the Divine Mercy Chaplet. It's important to pray for all souls in need of salvation, including those in Purgatory. The Divine Mercy Chaplet is a good prayer for this purpose. (The words of the chaplet are available online at TheDivineMercy. org.) What words or phrases in this prayer do I find most meaningful?

Prayer for the Journey

Dear Jesus:

So many things in life vie for my attention and seek to define me. It's so easy to let them: my job, my physicality, my money. And yet, everything I have, including my very life, is in your hands. Help me to stay vigilant in knowing that the only measure of wealth is in the love I give away. I must "die" to every other thing, even finally to my own self, before I may gaze upon your face and know my true worth. I will give you all, and you will redeem me. *Amen*.

STATION 13

Jesus Is Taken
Down from the Cross

A Scripture Reading

Now there was a virtuous and righteous man named Joseph who, though he was a member of the council, had not consented to their plan of action. He came from the Jewish town of Arimathea and was awaiting the kingdom of God. He went to Pilate and asked for the body of Jesus. After he had taken the body down, he wrapped it in a linen cloth and laid him in a rock-hewn tomb in which no one had yet been buried. It was the day of preparation, and the sabbath was about to begin. The women who had come from Galilee with him followed behind, and when they had seen the tomb and the way in which his body was laid in it, they returned and prepared spices and perfumed oils. Then they rested on the sabbath according to the commandment.

— Luke 23:50–56

A Moment to Reflect

The use of the lamb as a symbol of God's mercy can be traced to the beginning of Jewish history. Abraham's faithfulness is rewarded with a sacrificial ram, preventing the sacrifice of Isaac, his only son. In Exodus, the Jewish people are taught how they must prepare and consume a lamb so that their first-born sons might be "passed over" by the angel of death. The paschal lamb had to be a specific one set aside for sacrifice: an "unblemished" year-old male. At Jesus' birth in Bethlehem, we learn that he is wrapped in swaddling clothes, just like the lambs destined for sacrifice at Passover. The shepherds who prepared these lambs would have understood the correlation when they encountered the baby in the manger.

At the Last Supper, a Passover supper during the annual weeklong Feast of Unleavened Bread, Jesus tells his disciples: "Take it; this is my body" (Mk 14:22), and "This is my blood of the covenant, which will be shed for many" (Mk 14:24). In no uncertain terms, he was telling them that his was the body and blood to be sacrificed; he was the true Passover Lamb. And they must "do this"—eat his body and drink his blood—to be part of the new covenant that is being established. Would they have fully understood these strange words?

Perhaps those strange words took on new significance for the women and the other disciples as Jesus's lifeless body was taken down from the Cross and wrapped in linen, as he was at his birth, and laid in a tomb owned by of Joseph of Arimathea. Joseph was a wealthy, devout Jew who was also a secret follower of Jesus. He was a high-ranking member of the Sanhedrin court, but was outnumbered in the decision to execute Jesus. And so he chose to risk both his life and his reputation to retrieve Jesus' body for a proper Jewish burial. He would not leave Jesus' body on the Cross, to be picked at by birds and gawked at by passersby. His body would be buried according to Jewish custom, anointed with the myrrh and other spices the women at the crucifixion had hurriedly gathered as a final act of love. Their hopes had died. Only love remained.

My Creative Illuminations

Reread the gospel passage, taking note of the words and images that are particularly meaningful to you. Place yourself in the story, and feel the weight of the grief of those in the scene. You might choose to express these ideas creatively, using your favorite art supplies or a special notebook or journal. Once you have placed yourself in the story, take a few moments to reflect on the questions below.

"SURRENDER ALL" JOURNAL PROMPTS

Surrender to the weight of grief. Lifting someone who is sick, unconscious, or recently deceased is difficult; there is no life in the body, which becomes heavy. Am I experiencing some kind of spiritual grief or loss that needs to be brought to Jesus? How would I explain the "weight of grief" to someone who has never experienced it?

Recall that burying the dead is a corporal work of mercy. Joseph and the women would have had to touch a corpse on the Sabbath, breaking a Jewish rule. What made them willing to sidestep the law to care for Jesus' body? How does participating in the final rites and rituals of death benefit the soul?

What corporal work of mercy can I perform this week? How would I describe my experience afterward?

Be alive in Christ. Sometimes we attend Mass like people in a coma, offering no energy to the celebration. How might I better prepare for Mass so as to participate more intentionally and joyfully? Can I preview the gospel reading, or keep a Mass journal of thoughts the ceremony evokes in me?

TURN UP THE LIGHT

Consider how you might enter more fully into the experience of those who tended to the body of the crucified Christ by caring for someone who has died (or extend mercy to that person's family). You can do this by using your creative talents—perhaps drawing an image of a deceased loved one from an old photograph, or making a special card to ease someone's grief. Or you might physically tend to someone whose regular caregiver could use some relief: sit with an elderly parent and do a puzzle or give a manicure, or bring some cookies and have tea together. What act of mercy can you do today?

Prayer for the Journey

Dear Jesus:

All week long I shoulder the weight of my world, and it's hard to let that go and just rest. My mind continues to spin, keeping count of what's done and not done on my to-do list. I fail over and over again to give myself permission just to be. Call me to your stillness. Let me find silence so that I may know you are my God. *Amen.*

STATION 14

*Jesus Is
Laid in the Tomb*

Blessed
are they who
mourn
for they will
be
comforted
MATTHEW 5:4
JN

A Scripture Reading

Now a man was ill, Lazarus from Bethany, the village of Mary and her sister Martha. Mary was the one who had anointed the Lord with perfumed oil and dried his feet with her hair; it was her brother Lazarus who was ill. So the sisters sent word to him, saying, "Master, the one you love is ill." When Jesus heard this he said, "This illness is not to end in death, but is for the glory of God, that the Son of God may be glorified through it." . . .

Jesus told [Martha], "I am the resurrection and the life; whoever believes in me, even if he dies, will live, and everyone who lives and believes in me will never die. Do you believe this?" She said to him, "Yes, Lord. I have come to believe that you are the Messiah, the Son of God, the one who is coming into the world."

— John 11:1–4, 25–27

A Moment to Reflect

Once more we are in a garden, a place where life returns to its most basic and primitive state. Jesus is buried. He is like the grain of wheat that has died and fallen to the ground. His friends and followers were taught that this must happen for new life to spring forth, and they had witnessed many miracles over the last three years illustrating this. Yet this knowledge couldn't have diminished the very human sorrow and trauma experienced by the violent murder of their beloved teacher and friend.

This was new, uncharted territory. They must have been terrified that this could also happen to them. The promises of resurrection must have seemed far-fetched. Yes, Jesus had raised people from the dead. And yet, Lazarus and Jarius's daughter would face death again. So where is our hope? How do we believe?

It is hard to come to terms with death when we have not seen beyond it. We do not fully understand this wonderful kingdom of which Jesus speaks. Later, Paul would write about the wisdom of the kingdom, referencing the prophet Isaiah (see 64:3), "What eye has not seen, and ear has not heard, and what has not entered the human heart, what God has prepared for those who love him" (1 Cor 2:9). But Paul and the apostles had received the gift of the Holy Spirit by then. Now, by the tomb in this garden, all is silent. The Spirit has not been revealed, and there is only the bleakness of desolation. Any hope of new life must be taken on faith, learned by listening to the prophets and carefully studying the life of Jesus.

Take heart! Jesus will not leave us for long. He knows how hard it can be, how easily we are tempted to unbelief. When we are entombed in our own despair, Jesus Christ is not doing "nothing." There is something: a prodding at the edges of our souls, an invitation to walk through the darkness with him. A call.

After he was buried, Jesus "descended into hell" until the third day. This was not some added punishment for him. He clearly said on the Cross of his human mission, "It is finished" (Jn 19:30). Rather, it was to gather to himself all those held in the bondage of death, awaiting his light. Jesus is willing to reach down, beyond the grave, to the depths of our hell to find us where we are. Be still and listen for that undercurrent of the "peace of God that surpasses all understanding" (Phil 4:7)—and know that Jesus will call us from the tomb.

My Creative Illuminations

Reread the gospel passage, taking note of the words and images that are particularly meaningful to you. You might choose to express these ideas creatively, using your favorite art supplies or a special notebook or journal. Once you have placed yourself in the story, take a few moments to reflect on the questions below.

"SURRENDER ALL" JOURNAL PROMPTS

Surrender to the desolation. The disciples of Christ must have been bewildered by everything that had happened to their beloved Master. They probably felt totally numb as they received news of his death and burial. Have I experienced a similar period of desolation? Was I aware of God's presence? When I turned to God in prayer, did I find new hope?

Look once more at the artwork. The sun is setting on the crosses, and Jesus is entombed. The black outline around the stone here is in the form of the *omega*, the last letter of the Greek alphabet. This marks the end of his human life. But there is a slight purple glow around the stone, a bit of light peeking through. Something is happening. Jesus said he is "the Alpha and the Omega" (Rv 22:13). God's time is not linear, and the beginning and end are simultaneously "now." Can I imagine an eternity where love and salvation are not bound by time? What could I do if I didn't fear death?

Write a letter. If Jesus found me alone and desolate, what would he say to comfort me? What letter of consolation might my intimate friend, Jesus, write to me?

TURN UP THE LIGHT

"Faith is the realization of what is hoped for and evidence of things not seen" (Heb 11:1). How strong and active is your faith right now? Are you in need of a shot of new life? If you feel spiritually "stuck," or just feel the need to bring in some new life, try something new: check out an online community or podcast, make arrangements to attend an event at a local retreat center to learn about different prayer practices, or make a personal silent retreat.

Prayer for the Journey

Dear Jesus:

Your time is not linear, and death does not have the final word. Your love and saving power are present to me now and always. When I grow fearful in my limited understanding, help me to keep the faith and not give up. I want my very being to be an offering, poured out for your ever-loving kindness. Help me to use up every ounce of time, every talent, and all the earthly treasure you have bestowed on me to do your will, so that I may see your face shine upon me when my time is at hand. *Amen.*

In the Garden:
Resurrection!

JNORTON

the SPIRIT itself
Bears Witness with Our Spirit
that we are Children of God
and if children, then heirs
Heirs of God &
joint heirs with CHRIST
if only we suffer
with Him so that we may
also be glorified
with Him.

Romans 8:16-17

JN

A Scripture Reading

But Mary stayed outside the tomb weeping. And as she wept, she bent over into the tomb and saw two angels in white sitting there, one at the head and one at the feet where the body of Jesus had been. And they said to her, "Woman, why are you weeping?" She said to them, "They have taken my Lord, and I don't know where they laid him." When she had said this, she turned around and saw Jesus there, but did not know it was Jesus. Jesus said to her, "Woman why are you weeping? Whom are you looking for?"

—John 20:11–15a

A Moment to Reflect

The world offers all kinds of promises, comforts, and entice-ments. *Work hard enough, be good-looking or smart enough, and you'll find happiness.* In the end, we're never really satisfied. No matter how hard we strive, death still waits for each of us. Yet we also know that there is more: an eternal life where we are completely known and loved. Our lonely hearts seek the one true God, the Creator of all that is, seen and unseen.

Mary Magdalene knew what it was like to search for love. From scripture, we know that earlier in her life she was plagued with "seven demons" (Lk 8:2). They are never described, but we can take any one of the seven deadly sins and turn it into an addiction, a misguided attempt at finding peace and happiness, and imagine how tortured she was. Her unsatisfied heart was continually broken and lonely.

Then Jesus enters her life and she is transformed. Jesus sets things right again and restores order. The nature of the chains no longer matters because he has broken their hold and they have fallen away. With her burdens lifted, she is now willing and able to serve Jesus and his ministry with a light heart and spirit. With each act of service, she delves deeper into the mystery of this love.

Then, suddenly, everything is stripped away. Her world collapses once more as her liberator and teacher is crucified and buried. She ventures into his burial place to anoint his body, only to discover that the last concrete evidence of his presence is missing. Now what? How was she to cope with this new loss, feeling even more desperate for having once known his love?

But once we learn to walk with Jesus, he remains faithful. He doesn't abandon us to hopeless weeping. Our challenge, like Mary's, is to recognize him. She is oblivious to his presence until he calls her by name, "Mary." Sometimes the stories in our head seem more real than truth standing before us. Mary believed Jesus to be dead, so she did not recognize him as alive until he spoke to her heart in his familiar way. Eternity is carried in our name when spoken by the One who knows our soul.

Imagine a God who calls to us by name, whose gaze looks lovingly upon us and declares us "worthy" in spite of ourselves. A God who would surrender all to darkness so that we might understand his light. A God who became the very sacrifice of atonement for sin so that he may offer each of us grace—the forgiveness we don't deserve. He offers us a love *that* big! What does he ask in return? That we love one another in the pouring out of self, as he loved us. That we put aside our own desires and need for control and follow him. He asks us to surrender all for love.

My Creative Illuminations

Reread the gospel passage, taking note of the words and images that are particularly meaningful to you. You might choose to express these ideas creatively, using your favorite art supplies or a special notebook or journal. Once you have placed yourself in the story, take a few moments to reflect on the questions below.

"SURRENDER ALL" JOURNAL PROMPTS

Where do I discover Jesus? Mary doesn't recognize the risen Jesus at first, even after knowing him so well in life. How might he have changed form? Why might her perception not have allowed her to see him at first? Have I ever had an experience in life where I looked back and recognized the presence of Jesus only in hindsight? Did it make me want to be more aware to the possibility of his presence going forward?

How do I seek Jesus? In St. John Paul II's address at the fifteenth World Youth Day on August 18, 2000, he said:

It is Jesus that you seek when you dream of happiness. He is waiting for you when nothing else you find satisfies you. He is the beauty to which you are so attracted. It is he who provoked you with that thirst for fullness that will not let you settle for compromise. It is he who urges you to shed the masks of the false life; it is he who reads in your heart your most genuine choices, the choices that others try to stifle. It is Jesus who stirs in you the desire to do something great with your lives; the will to follow an ideal, the refusal to allow yourself to be ground down by mediocrity, the courage to commit yourselves humbly and patiently to improving yourselves and society, making the world more human and more fraternal.

What words or lines of this quote resonate with me?

Am I ready for resurrection? How has God spoken my name? Where have I heard him call to me most clearly? Is there anything that I am holding on to, afraid to let go, that prevents me from running after him? Love is not a feeling, but an action— what does this mean to me?

TURN UP THE LIGHT

The book of Revelation, particularly chapter 21, has some beautiful images of what heaven will be like. Imagine "what eye has not seen and ear has not heard" (1 Cor 2:9). Write down or make a piece of art about some of heaven's imagined qualities. Look at them when you are tempted to selfishness to remind you to surrender your will for God's promise.

Prayer for the Journey

Dear Jesus:

Help me to grow in your love and to surrender all for your kingdom. You are not a distant God, remotely judging and condemning from afar. You are a personal God, alive in me. You call me by name. You created me, and all people, to share the same breath of spirit and the same dignity, which you have bestowed upon us from conception. When I am tempted to think too highly of myself, relying on my own understanding and worried about worldly opinions, remind me that in you I am already enough. When I am tempted to judge others, let me recall that I do not have that authority. I cannot be separated from your love, unless I choose to be. Help me do your will. *Amen.*

Acknowledgments

Writing this book gave me a chance to pause and reflect on each part of the story that we as Catholics tell and retell when we walk the Stations of the Cross. Diving deeper into these mysteries helped me to better understand that Jesus' Passion is how God proves his love to us so its significance can never be lost, no matter how much the world changes.

I'd like to express my deep appreciation for my family, who help me to experience God's love in human form as well: My daughter, Emma. I loved you before you were born and every day since, even the hard ones. Maybe especially the hard ones because, looking back, I can see that's where I really learned to love unconditionally.

To my husband, Anthony. I'm not sure either of us fully knew what we were doing when we walked down the aisle long ago. But we put God first, and we have not walked alone. I love you for being a solid rock in my life and for supporting my crazy art aspirations for the last thirty years. Hopefully I have done the same for you.

To Phyllis and Marilyn: Each of you has been a model of unwavering faith and service at different stages of my life. Momma, you planted my roots on fertile ground. And Marilyn, you helped shaped the branches of my faith. I wouldn't be writing this book without your example of unselfish love.

I am grateful to the whole Ave team for reaching out to me about this book project. I am grateful that they saw something special in this series and saw ways to take it further and deeper than I ever imagined.

I would also like to thank those who produced Divine Mercy resources I referenced in this book: *Divine Mercy in*

My Soul by St. Maria Faustina Kowalska (Marian Press 2003), and TheDivineMercy.org. I cannot remember a time when the world was in such dire need of the merciful touch of Jesus. Thank you sharing the life and writings of St. Faustina Kowalska.

Reflections for Walking the Stations

Many Catholic churches have the Stations of the Cross prominently displayed—either along the walls of the nave or outside. Use these short reflections to enter more deeply into your prayer walk. They may be read in a group setting (aloud) or on your own (silently).

STATION 1:   Jesus Is Condemned to Death
Jesus is questioned, accused, and bound;
an innocent man condemned; crowded,
All alone.

STATION 2:   Jesus Takes Up His Cross
He is bruised and bloodied and spit-on;
The burden of sin accepted; heart trembles,
Death looms.

STATION 3:   Jesus Falls the First Time
The weight crushes, heart pounds;
His breath is labored, legs shake and bend;
Bone hits stone, pain sears.

STATION 4:   Jesus Meets His Mother
Sorrow overwhelms;
Hearts are pierced by bloodied thorns;
Love strengthens resolve.

STATION 5:   Jesus Meets Simon of Cyrene
Called out from the crowd;
Dissonance to harmony;
Pain lifted, weight shared.

STATION 6: Veronica Wipes the Face of Jesus
Blood washed away, love remains;
Compassion freely given;
Behold, His image.

STATION 7: Jesus Falls the Second Time
Faith dims, so alone;
Gravity pulls like a stone;
Must I rise? Can I?

STATION 8: Jesus Meets the Women of Jerusalem
Caring eyes, tears fall;
Compassion freely flows;
Strength comes through pain shared.

STATION 9: Jesus Falls the Third Time
Falling again, crushed;
The end is near, Father help me;
This Cross too great to bear.

STATION 10: Jesus Is Stripped of His Garments
Disrobed and laid bare;
Humiliated and sole possessions gone.
Untorn.

STATION 11: Jesus Is Nailed to the Cross
Pounding agony; arms stretched wide,
Embrace is empty; forsaken by God.
Stay with me.

STATION 12: Jesus Dies
Darkness consumes all;
Body spent, veil torn in two;
Finished.

STATION 13: Jesus Is Taken Down from the Cross
Lifeless, lifted down;
Wrapped in mercy, placed in tomb;
Women watch and weep.

STATION 14: Jesus Is Laid in the Tomb
Behind the stone, darkness;
Descent to blackness, lightless, hell.
But wait.

STATION 15: Resurrection!
Heavy stone rolled back;
Angels speak of light and truth;
Women run in Joy!